CAPES AND ACCESSORIES

A BOOK ABOUT SUPERPOWERS

ASSIA EL MOUSSAWI

Capes and Accessories
Copyright © 2022 by Assia El Moussawi

All rights reserved. No part of this publication may be reproduced, distributed, or transmitted in any form or by any means, including photocopying, recording, or other electronic or mechanical methods, without the prior written permission of the author, except in the case of brief quotations embodied in critical reviews and certain other non-commercial uses permitted by copyright law.

Tellwell Talent
www.tellwell.ca

ISBN
978-0-2288-6954-2 (Hardcover)
978-0-2288-6725-8 (Paperback)

for the little boy with big Dreams, Jude...
For Mom and Dad who gave me wings to fly...
And for my best friend and husband Bassem,
I couldn't have done it without you!

Hello there, I am Eva! my mom told me that I am a special girl, and I agree! and it is not just due to my beautiful hair. Do you really want to know the actual reason? Ok, here we go...

Mommy believes that I am courageous enough to put my noise cancelling headphones on whenever I am overwhelmed by loud sounds.

While I am unable to formulate words with great sense, I ensure that you can understand what I am trying to say in my own way.
Just because I struggle to make eye contact does not mean I can't see you.
I might not always succeed, but giving my best shot every single time is a special talent of mine.

Hi!, I am Lukas. I move around in a wheelchair, due to my inability to walk, but do you know what I like best in the entire world?

Besides chocolate ice cream, of course? And waffles? To be challenged to a race and show off my speed!!

Yes!!! because I am super-fast when riding my super wheelchair and I am definitely a winner!
I like to have fun, enjoy a good laugh, and giggle just like you!
And that my friend, is what makes me special.

I can't see you, but guess what? I can feel you...
I can sense your curious eyes casting a glance at me and wondering how I manage to do everything.
You want to know what my superpower is and what makes me special?

I can do everything even when I am unable to see a thing because that does not stop me from enjoying a life filled with fun, frolic, and adventure!
Here is another superpower of mine: I can pick my nose without anyone noticing a thing!

Super cool, right?

All it means is that I put in extra effort to do what you do, which makes me a fighter all the way, and SUPER SPECIAL!
Here is another secret you may want to know about. I won the first place in the spelling competition at school!!

Hmm, impressive, right?

I am Lina...

I struggle to focus and pay attention, I am **super** active! and feel a compelling need to keep moving! That is how I function. If you see me in the supermarket, I am the one who is always struggling to stay in the line and wait for my turn!

On the other hand, if you see me at school, I am the one who is always interrupting conversations and always moving around. I can't control it, but I am always trying my best, and this what makes me special.

This is who I am, **Super Lina.**

I am Adam... I run, I talk, and I burp!

Once my mom said that life is not always fair to people. This is exactly why we must always be compassionate and caring to all.
I was wondering what makes me special, My cool haircut maybe?

Mommy said that I am special because I never stop smiling and I am always kind to others, but can you guess what is it that really makes me super special?
I befriend those with superpowers! Not with only capes, they come with different accessories as well!!

Have you ever wondered what would this world look like if everything in it was of the same colour? How about if all your fingers were all similar?

Or you and your friends were alike? Can you imagine what would happen if the planets in the solar system would be the same?

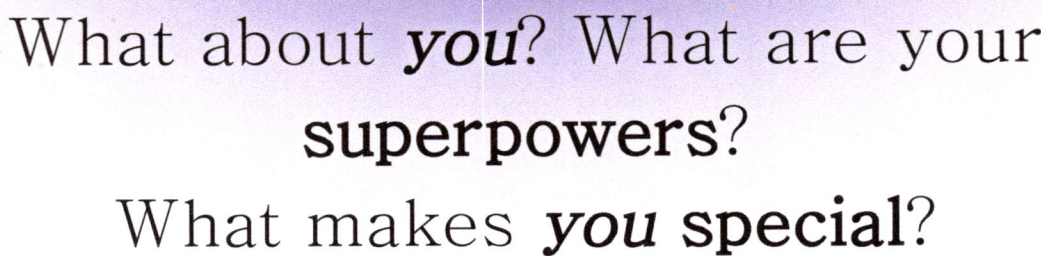

What about *you*? What are your **superpowers**? What makes *you* **special**?

_____